praise for Infinity

"This play is as brilliant as it is haunting—a perfect combination of music, math and science that doesn't make your head hurt, but manages to makes your heart hurt."
—*The Theatre Reader*

NNNN. "Brilliant: makes you feel as much as it makes you think."
—Susan G. Cole, *NOW Magazine*

"It's a fascinating subject that affects us all—time, dealing with it; coping with it. Seeing *Infinity* is one way of using your time wisely."
—*The Slotkin Letter*

★ ★ ★ ½
"Moscovitch . . . is visceral. Extremely affecting."
—Carly Maga, *Toronto Star*

★ ★ ★
—Kelly Nestruck, *The Globe and Mail*

★ ★ ★ ★
—*Theatromania*

Infinity

also by Hannah Moscovitch

East of Berlin
Little One & Other Plays
The Russian Play & Other Short Works
This Is War

Infinity

by Hannah Moscovitch

with original music
by Njo Kong Kie

Playwrights Canada Press
Toronto

Infinity © Copyright 2017 by Hannah Moscovitch
All music © Copyright 2017 by Njo Kong Kie

No part of this book may be reproduced, downloaded, or used in any form or by any means without the prior written permission of the publisher, except for excerpts in a review or by a licence from Access Copyright, www.accesscopyright.ca.

For professional or amateur production rights, please contact:
Ian Arnold at Catalyst TCM
310-100 Broadview Ave., Toronto, ON M4M 3H3
416.645.0935 :: info@catalysttcm.com

For music rights, please contact info@musicpicnic.com.

LIBRARY AND ARCHIVES CANADA CATALOGUING IN PUBLICATION
Moscovitch, Hannah, author
    Infinity / Hannah Moscovitch.

A play.
Issued in print and electronic formats.
ISBN 978-1-77091-734-7 (paperback).--ISBN 978-1-77091-735-4 (pdf).--
ISBN 978-1-77091-736-1 (epub).--ISBN 978-1-77091-737-8 (mobi)

    I. Title.

PS8626.O837I54 2017   C812'.6   C2016-907312-2
                                          C2016-907313-0

We acknowledge the financial support of the Canada Council for the Arts, the Ontario Arts Council (OAC), the Ontario Media Development Corporation, and the Government of Canada through the Canada Book Fund for our publishing activities.

To my son, Elijah Barry.

Time goes by itself. If you listen sometimes you can hear it.
—John Mighton, *The Little Years*

"But the number of men who make a definite contribution to anything whatsoever is very small," he said, pausing by the pear tree . . .
—Virginia Woolf, *To the Lighthouse*

Sobering just how horrible two very nice people can end up in a relationship that plays to both their weaknesses.
—Alain de Botton

The Theatre of the Infinite
Lee Smolin

Our insatiability condemns us forever to seek the infinite from the finite.
—Roberto Mangabeira Unger, *The Religion of the Future*

The story that we tell is that there have been art and science for as long as we have been human. And I am inclined to believe it, as there is evidence for it. We've been painting on cave walls for at least twenty thousand years, and we could have been painting on other less well-preserved surfaces for much longer. The cave paintings don't look like the works of beginners. Of course, reconstructing the past is hard and the intense curiosity we feel for our origins tempts us to give in to fantasy and projection. An iconic *New Yorker* cartoon shows a female cave painter queried by her apprentice, "Does it strike anyone else as weird that none of the great painters have been men?"* And indeed, here we face the limits of knowledge of the past, for how will we ever know?

The same caves yield bones on which patterns of lines have been carved. As first reported by Alexander Marshack, these recordings come in groups of seven, fourteen, or fifteen, twenty-eight or twenty-nine. Marshack took this to be evidence for early astronomers tracking the

---

* http://imgc-cn.artprintimages.com/images/P-473-488-90/61/6150/PXCG100Z/

lunar cycle, but he never mentioned an obvious and equally plausible interpretation according to which our cave painting ancestors practised contraception. And, indeed, how will we ever know which interpretation of the past is right? It is even possible that they were trying to work out a reason for the coincidence of those two cycles—a legitimate and open question to this day.

I would love to know what these early scientists talked about with the early artists, as they sat around the fire, drinking early beer. I suspect that, then as now, a lot of it was gossip—but did they also wonder about their origins or their future? Could they have put their heads together and imagined us? For, the paleontologists tell us, we are the same creatures as them. All that separates us is eight hundred generations of progress in art and science.

I like to think of scientists and artists as explorers of our common future, laying down tracks in the domains of nature and the imagination. In addition to these two frontiers, our future is marked by the frontiers of society and of spirituality; these are the domains of politics and religion. These four domains and those who explore them have a special and permanent place in human society.

When the explorers of these four frontiers are in conversation, our culture has a chance to grow coherently into the future. When, as now, physicists have no idea what biologists talk about—let alone what the issues are on the frontier of painting or photography—the culture is incoherent. Indeed, it is impossible to know how people in a century or two will think of us, but my best bet is that ours will be known as the era of missed opportunities.

For the last century we have lived in a culture in which everyone wants to be an artist—or at least live like one. College students dress in informal fashions pioneered by the artists who worked in Paris in the early twentieth century or in SoHo and Tribeca in the 1960s and 1970s, when those neighbourhoods were the domain of poor artists squatting in converted industrial spaces. Now their lofts are the homes of lawyers and investment bankers, never mind that the spaces themselves—a single wall of windows facing a dark cave—may have made great painting studios but are awkward to arrange as an apartment in a city whose building code requires that every bedroom have a window.

But the fashion is changing, for now geeks are cool. It is possible to imagine that soon everyone will want to live the lifestyle of a scientist or engineer. That will certainly be convenient for the corporations of the world, because we geeks work all the time. At some software companies there are technical updates posted strategically in the bathrooms, so as not to lose those private minutes to private thoughts. There was a time the best jobs came with an expectation of being able to take long alcoholic lunches and leave work for golf or a sail at three p.m. Now the coolest jobs available to recent grads are patterned on the lives of obsessive, pale MIT graduate students who never leave the limits of the infinite corridor.

At this moment then, there is a special poignancy when artists seek to portray the lives of scientists. Sometimes this is just a very contemporary form of camp, as in the attractively dressed young female scientists who have become a staple of bad movies and television series, who squint seriously while they come up with the idea that saves the day but never seem to encounter the real issues that face women scientists in the still male-dominated scientific workplace.

But occasionally an artist attempts a serious portrayal of science. Theatre seems to offer an opportunity for this. This subject has been taken up in recent years by Michael Frayn's *Copenhagen*, David Auburn's *Proof*, Steve Martin's *Picasso at the Lapin Agile*, and Alan Alda's portrayal of Richard Feynman in Peter Parnell's play *QED*. In 2014 we had films about Alan Turing and Stephen Hawking.

That same year, I was extremely fortunate to be asked to advise on the production of a truly great new play about scientists: Hannah Moscovitch's *Infinity*, which was produced by Ross Manson's Volcano company and premiered in the spring of 2015 at Toronto's Tarragon Theatre. *Infinity* is a three-character play about a violinist and composer who marries a theoretical physicist and together have a daughter, and a mathematician who struggles with romantic relationships. It had forty-five sold-out performances and won the Dora Mavor Moore Award for best new play of the Toronto season.

Seven years ago Manson commissioned Moscovitch, who was at the beginning of a rapidly ascending career, to write a play about time, for him to direct. For five years they developed the play in workshop with a quartet of top-notch performers (four because the composer's music, composed by Njo Kong Kie, was, for the premiere, played by violinist Andréa Tyniec, while her character was portrayed by actor Amy Rutherford). At some point they got a hold of my book *Time Reborn*, and Manson asked me to meet with Moscovitch and advise her and the company on the production.

I am the son of a playwright, Pauline Smolin, so this was an invitation I respected and appreciated. I had grown up partly in the theatre world; my first play was when my mother took me to see Joseph Papp's *Medea* as part of Shakespeare in the Park, when I was perhaps five.

Meeting Hannah Moscovitch was a privilege and a thrill. Smart, quick-witted, charismatic, and kind, she probed my ideas on time and how we physicists live during a coffee that stretched for hours and continued in email correspondence.

Months later, the director invited me to a reading, which took place on a cold and icy Toronto winter's day. I was stunned by the play and the strong cast members. Afterwards the assistant director noticed I needed a haircut and immediately produced scissors and gave me one. This is something that would never happen in a physics department. There is no avoiding the fact that it is way more fun hanging out with theatre people than physicists. As Manson said at one point, "Everyone in this production is brilliant," and there is—and, I suspect, has been for twenty thousand years—nothing like the company of smart artists.

Moscovitch's play is about the great gulfs between the past, present, and future. It is about how the past is unrecoverable while, at the same time, it moulds us. We can't know what our parents said to each other when they met, but their history is, to a larger extent than we can easily admit, our future. It is about how time shapes us as lovers, spouses, and parents, and as the children of those parents. And it is also about the idea of time, as it is understood by musicians and physicists.

In turn I invited the company to spend a day at Perimeter Institute for Theoretical Physics, where I work. The actors who were to play the physicist and mathematician, Paul Braunstein and Haley McGee, watched us like hawks. Amy Rutherford remarked to me how attractive and charismatic she found the people she met, with their evident intelligence and focus. The designer, Teresa Przybylski, queried our peculiar dress habits. Months later when I saw the opening it was clear they understood us. Physicists can recognize each other across an airport, as can mathematicians, and their characters would pass.

Somehow Moscovitch caught precisely our particular intensity. Her mathematician has all the quirky literalness and childlike inappropriateness of the best of those I've met. And she gets in trouble in ways common to smart academics.

One of the truest moments in the play comes when Carmen, the musician, confronts her husband, Elliot, the physicist, who has left their bed at three a.m. to work.

ELLIOT: Listen, I'll stop now, I'm finished my . . . PhD—and I will . . . stop now, I said I would and I . . . meant it when I said it.

CARMEN: Yeah?

ELLIOT: Yeah.

Beat.

CARMEN: *Can* you stop?

ELLIOT: Yes.

CARMEN: Can you?

Silence as ELLIOT considers the question.

Can you?

ELLIOT: *(shrugs)* Maybe . . . maybe . . . look, maybe . . . ? I don't know—I don't know: yeah, I . . . don't know. I like to work, it yeah—it gives me something—I have this sense that I can contribute something that's . . . substantial and I want to—I don't know, sometimes, it almost surfaces. And my PhD was . . . I did feel relief, and I . . . know the department was . . . happy with it, but I don't think I went far enough with it—

CARMEN: You unified string theory and loop quantum gravity / using—

ELLIOT: I—yes—I know, fine, good, yes, but it's limited. Like I can't broaden my... I have this sense that it's just out of reach, I don't know, it's... bothering me, it's... and I feel like if I keep going, I'll get there.

> *Beat.*

And that thought, it's... not leaving me alone.

> *Beat.*

(hesitating) Yeah...

> *Beat.*

I—yeah—if I'm being—if I'm being... very—I *do* still have something to... prove.

> *Pause.*

CARMEN: Elliot?

ELLIOT: Yeah?

CARMEN: You know that when I talk to the secretary of the Harvard physics department she tells me that they've never had a PhD candidate who's as talented as you in the whole time she's been the secretary—which is thirty-seven years.

> *Beat.*

Did you know that?

> *ELLIOT nods.*

It . . . doesn't make it . . . better?

    ELLIOT *shakes his head.*

ELLIOT: No.

CARMEN: No, hunh.

    Michael Frayn's *Copenhagen* is also a well-written three-hander. I saw the play in London, and while the characters on the stage were called Niels Bohr and Werner Heisenberg, they were not physicists. They were at best professors of English or history at Cambridge. Moscovitch's characters are us.
    They are at the same time very much her characters. Moscovitch's Elliot is not me, and his problems, as the play reveals them, are, thankfully, not mine. But, most remarkably, during the course of the play he changes his mind about a key question that faces contemporary physics, which is the nature of time. And his change of mind is exactly one I made over the last decade, which led to my writing *Time Reborn*.
    The question at the heart of physics is whether time, particularly the present moment and its place in a flow of moments, is fundamental or an illusion. Einstein and most theorists since see time as an emergent, reducible concept. What is real, they claim, is not the present moment, but the whole history of the universe, taken as one, as a single timeless entity. Within this frozen history, there is no fundamental difference between past, present, and future. All three are equally present in the frozen "block universe," so the difference is just a matter of perspective; "then" and "now" are no different from "here" and "there."
    For reasons that I had explained in *Time Reborn*, and in my book *The Singular Universe and the Reality of Time*, written with Roberto Mangabeira Unger, I have come via a long, painful process to reject this received wisdom in favour of the view that time is fundamental. This view asserts that what is real is the present moment and the processes of change and causation lead to the creation of the new moment out of the present.

In *Infinity*, Moscovitch captures this change of mind not only as an intellectual process but also its implications for the character and his understanding of his life, as a scientist as well as a husband and father.

I had tried to express these personal implications of our conception of time in the epilogue of *Time Reborn*. There I wrote that our conception of time shapes how we understand society's greatest challenges, such as climate change, as well as our most personal struggles, with parenthood, anxiety, ambition, and responsibility. In a short play, Moscovitch communicated these insights much better than I had been able to. Each time I saw the play I was shocked and moved.

Towards the end of the creative process, Moscovitch and Manson asked me to supply Elliot's scientific biography, which they used as the backstory for the final version. So, with their permission, I attributed to Elliot achievements that I at one time aspired to, and still do, but which for now remain unrealized hopes, like the unification of string theory with loop quantum gravity (which became his PhD thesis). But it was completely Moscovitch who understood that the issue of whether time is real or illusion is at once a pressing scientific problem, a question a composer must address, and a question for all of us professionals who also aim to be good parents, who love both our children and our work. She portrayed the inner conflict felt by those who are drawn by our passions and loves to each other, while at the same time drawn away from each other by other passions and loves we imagine are timeless.

And she also understands that time is a central problem for art to resolve at this confused moment, when modernism has given way to postmodernism. That is, a pretense at timelessness has been replaced by a pretense of ephemeralness. This, in turn, is giving way to novel ways to communicate the truths we live out, as we struggle with the same questions those first artists and scientists might have talked over, back when the possibility of representing an animal in flight with some pigment brushed onto a rock was shocking and new.

"The Theatre of the Infinite" was originally published in *Art Practical* 7.2, October 2015.

Lee Smolin is a theoretical physicist who has been since 2001 a founding and senior faculty member at Perimeter Institute for Theoretical Physics. His main contributions have been so far to the quantum theory of gravity, to which he has been a co-inventor and major contributor to two major directions, loop quantum gravity and deformed special relativity. He has also contributed to quantum field theory, the foundations of quantum mechanics, theoretical biology, and the philosophy of science and economics. He is the author of more than 150 scientific papers and numerous essays and writings for the public on science. He is an adjunct professor of physics at the University of Waterloo and a member of the graduate faculty of the philosophy department at the University of Toronto.

Infinity was co-produced by Tarragon Theatre and Volcano in the Extraspace at Tarragon from March 25 to May 3, 2015, with the following cast and creative team:

Paul Braunstein: Elliot
Haley McGee: Sarah Jean
Amy Rutherford: Carmen
with Andréa Tyniec on violin

Composer and Music Director: Njo Kong Kie
Director: Ross Manson
Choreographer: Kate Alton
Lighting Design: Rebecca Picherack
Set and Costume Design: Teresa Przybylski
Stage Manager: Isabelle Ly

Punctuation.

Dash (—): a dash at the end of a line of dialogue indicates a cut-off
Dash 2 (—): a dash in the middle of a line of dialogue indicates a quick change in thought or a stutter
Ellipsis (. . .): an ellipsis at the end of a line indicates a trail off
Ellipsis 2 (. . .): an ellipsis in the middle of a line indicates a hesitation or a mental search for a thought or a word
Ellipsis 3 (. . . dialogue . . .): ellipses on either side of a line of dialogue indicates that the person who is speaking is doing so over the other character or trying to interrupt the other character
Slash (/): a slash indicates the point at which the character that speaks next interrupts the character that is currently speaking

Beat: approximately a one-count
Pause: approximately a three-count
Silence: approximately a six-count

Notes.

Time, place, and memory in the play can be created with light, sound, choreography, props, and small hints of furniture. Nothing naturalist. The stage can be cluttered or empty but it should have open dark space in some places so that characters can emerge and recede into blackness.

Music.

The music in the play is composed for solo violin by Njo Kong Kie. It was written for, and integral to, the original production and remount at the Tarragon Theatre. It is encouraged that future productions use the same music. For further information about acquiring performance rights, please contact Ian Arnold at Catalyst TCM (416.645.0935, info@catalysttcm.com), and for information about acquiring music rights and the performance edition of the score, please contact info@musicpicnic.com.

Characters.

Sarah Jean (*various ages; a little girl of eight years old to midtwenties*)
Elliot (*various ages; midtwenties to midthirties*)
Carmen (*various ages; midtwenties to midthirties*)

The names of the characters in this play are not intended to limit casting to any particular ethnic group. Casting should reflect the diversity of the country where the play is being produced.

Overture.

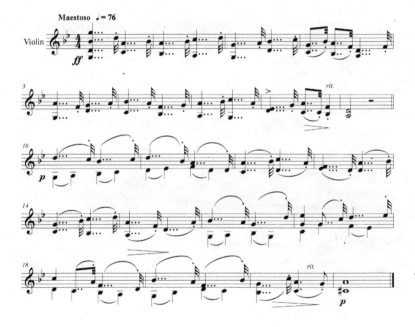

Act One.
Scene One.

SARAH JEAN stands there, considering, looking at us, twitching her hand.

Finally, she speaks to us.

SARAH JEAN: On the way home in the cab, I was uh—uh crying, and the cab driver smiled at me and said: "Love?" I said: "You picked me up in front of a funeral home; so, no." Then I thought about it and I said: "People do that? They sit in your cab and cry over love? That seems a little . . . much to me."

Beat.

He turned and gave me a surprised look.

SARAH JEAN considers, twitching her hand.

And now I can't stop . . . thinking that . . .

Beat.

SARAH JEAN twitches the fingers on her hand.

(very low) Fuck.

Beat.

The thing is: two weeks ago, a friend of mine, my . . . big blond American friend, from Iowa, said this thing to me about . . . what I'm like, and . . . I'm trying to think if—if it's—if she's . . .

Pause. Thinking.

She said that—that I'm . . . uh, uh, fucked up . . . about love . . . which . . . ?

Pause. Thinking.

Which I don't think is . . . ? I've had lots of good . . . ? I'm very normal.

Transition.

Allegro.

Scene Two.

We're in a small room off of a party, where partygoers have left their coats. Perhaps there's a coat rack. Indie hipster music is playing, off. CARMEN is putting on her coat, holding a wine glass with red wine in it that's nearly empty now. ELLIOT enters. CARMEN looks at ELLIOT for a split second. The split second after CARMEN *looks away,* ELLIOT *smiles. (This will only be visible in small houses.) As* ELLIOT *says the lines below,* CARMEN *isn't looking at or paying attention to* ELLIOT *at all: she's draining and putting down her wine glass, pulling on a winter jacket and gloves, finding her keys in her handbag, etc. All* CARMEN's *conduct should suggest she's about to leave the party.*

ELLIOT: I couldn't catch your eye in the kitchen. I'm Elliot, I . . . came in here: I want to meet you.

CARMEN: Why?

Beat.

ELLIOT: I . . . asked about you, I asked the other people at the party, and I found out your name's Carmen and . . . you're single.

Pause.

CARMEN: I'm—yeah. I'm . . . yeah. I'm single.

ELLIOT: Yeah?

CARMEN: I just broke up with my fiancé.

Beat.

ELLIOT: How's that . . . going?

CARMEN *turns and looks at him, hostile.*

I'm not . . . joking: I'm trying to find out if . . . y . . . ?

CARMEN: What?

ELLIOT: *(new tack)* Can I ask: why did you break up with him?

CARMEN: I stopped loving him.

ELLIOT: Well, *yeah:* but why?

Pause as CARMEN thinks, hard; then:

CARMEN: I . . . don't know. I don't know: he's not a shithead, he's . . . ! He's very kind, and I'm not saying he's not masculine. He grew up on a farm, he drives tractors and . . . snowmobiles—I met him in high school, in the library; he was failing math, and a lot of subjects, and I helped him out. I didn't tutor him, I taught him to cheat, and he asked me to senior prom: I lost my virginity to him, prom night, like a cheerleader, and then I lived out on his family's farm for a while and they were so kind to me and then I got into Harvard and moved here and we've been—I don't know . . . I don't know.

ELLIOT: Is it because he's stupid?

CARMEN regards ELLIOT curiously and with some hostility because she's just realized that it's probably true: her ex-fiancé was stupid. She twitches her fingers as she thinks about it.

You hadn't uh . . . ? You hadn't . . . ? That hadn't occurred to you?

CARMEN: No.

Silence as CARMEN twitches her fingers and thinks. She forgets about ELLIOT for a moment. ELLIOT watches her.

ELLIOT: What's that twitch?

CARMEN looks at her hand.

CARMEN: *(twitching it)* That?

ELLIOT: Yeah.

> CARMEN *looks at her hand, twitches it more slowly.*

It's a scale.

CARMEN: Yeah.

ELLIOT: I like musicians.

CARMEN: Why?

ELLIOT: Uh—

CARMEN: You like *music*.

ELLIOT: Uh no, no, it's not the music, it's that musicians know about time. They . . . have a . . . sense of what time is, that it . . . doesn't exist, that it . . . slides, and that's something most people don't understand: you know, Einstein's dictum that the distinction between past, present, and future is merely a very persistent illusion.

> *Beat.*

And how musicians talk—they speak in intervals, they use a lot of timekeeping terminology—

CARMEN: *I* don't.

ELLIOT: You probably do.

CARMEN: No, I don't.

> ELLIOT *smiles, changes the topic.*

ELLIOT: This morning, on campus, I asked a composer for his thoughts on time. He said that time, in music, divides the genius from the dilettante. He said, "Taste and tastelessness exist side by side on the continuum: they're divided by the length of a pause." He asked me if I'd read Adorno on time. I said no. He said: "You should." I asked him if he'd read Einstein on time. He said: "No." I said: "Oh skip it."

CARMEN smiles.

I think I picked him up, actually, uh . . . I was so . . . interested in what he was saying, it seemed . . . sexual to him, I think . . . Time is also the dividing line between genius and the abyss in theoretical physics, but it all comes down to *time*, time spent on research—

CARMEN: You're a theoretical physicist.

ELLIOT: I'm—yeah—I'm doing a PhD in theoretical physics.

CARMEN smiles.

CARMEN: How specialized is it?

ELLIOT: It—it—why?

CARMEN: I'm trying to picture what you do.

ELLIOT: I'm working on a theory of well, uh, uh, *everything*.

CARMEN: Everything.

ELLIOT: Yeah, it's—yeah—it's not a field of study that goes in for much humility. But in particular my work, because . . . I'm trying to . . . unify all physics. I recently proved explicitly the two-loop finiteness of string theory. That means that to the third order of an approximation scheme the theory has no problem with infinities. And now I'm working on solving the Wheeler-DeWitt equation, which is a mathematical attempt to combine the ideas of quantum mechanics and general relativity.

CARMEN tries hard to reckon with what he just said.

ELLIOT watches this, then:

It—yeah: it's specialized, but it—it *is* fulfilling, in some larger sense. I—sometimes I—this'll probably sound . . . stupid, but I stand in . . . the lab and listen to the atoms and they sound . . .

Beat.

CARMEN: Like what?

ELLIOT: *(reaching to describe it)* Sometimes it's like . . . a kind of . . . everything. Sometimes it's more like a dull ache: longing . . .

CARMEN: They sound lonely?

ELLIOT: *(realizing it's true)* Yyyyeahhh . . .

CARMEN: The atoms are lonely.

ELLIOT: *(grinning)* Yep.

CARMEN: Are you . . . ? You're . . . spending a lot of time by yourself?

ELLIOT: Yeah.

ELLIOT and CARMEN grin at each other.

There is a sudden animal stillness between them: attraction.

CARMEN: There are a lot of pretty girls out in the kitchen.

ELLIOT: You're very pretty.

CARMEN: Yeah?

ELLIOT: Plus most of those girls are in the Social Thought department: they say things like: "*Science is just another language.*" I don't want to date them, I want to give them a seminar on the philosophical implications of their stupidity. No: you know what? I don't know why. But I am certain it's you I . . . want.

There is a still beat between ELLIOT *and* CARMEN. *Then* ELLIOT *moves towards* CARMEN. CARMEN *leans in.* ELLIOT *holds* CARMEN, *kisses her—delicate but with hunger.* CARMEN *breaks off the kiss.*

CARMEN: I just—wait: whoever you are—

ELLIOT: Elliot.

CARMEN: *(unaware of her exact use of time)* Elliot, I left my fiancé two days ago so I can probably offer you fifteen to twenty minutes of sex, followed by forty-five minutes of crying. That's the ratio of sex to crying I have to offer right now.

Pause as ELLIOT *smiles.*

Why are you smiling?

ELLIOT: You're using . . .

CARMEN: I'm oh—I'm using timekeeping terminology. I'm—yeah—I'm a violinist, and a master's student . . . of music composition. And yeah okay: I do think of music as a . . . sculpture in time.

Silence: they look at each other, grinning. Then ELLIOT *and* CARMEN *kiss again: passionate, mutual. There's an escalation of sexuality, sexy, then:*

Transition.

Interlude Act One Scene Two–Three.

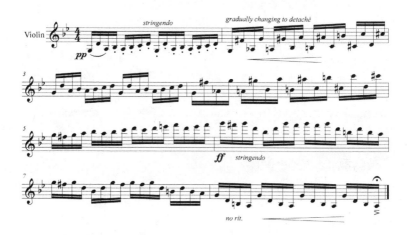

Scene Three.

SARAH JEAN thinks and thinks: she's considering: am I fucked up about love? Then abruptly she turns and speaks to us.

SARAH JEAN: Okay, for example: here's a good one. When I was at Harvard, I dated a mathematician for almost a year. He was a very good mathematician. We'd take our clothes off, and have some sex, and that'd be bracketed by doing mathematics on both sides. He was . . . It was appealing to be with him because . . . I'd finally found someone who thought how I thought. I had a lot of blackboards up on the walls of my apartment and he'd be naked, yelling at me about mathematics, and scribbling his arguments down on the blackboards. He broke a lot of chalk. There was a lot of chalk dust in his pubic hair.

SARAH JEAN stops waxing romantic and becomes worried about herself.

I was nineteen years old at the time. He was thirty-six, and married. He was also my teacher and famous.

SARAH JEAN considers.

She gets a little more worried about herself, and a little defensive.

Hunh, okay maybe that one's not . . . as good . . . an example as I thought.

Transition.

Interlude Act One Scene Three–Four.

Scene Four.

We're in a public washroom. CARMEN *is holding a pregnancy stick. There are pregnancy kit instructions and a torn-open pregnancy kit box lying on the ground.* CARMEN *stares at the stick, unblinking, seething.* ELLIOT *looks at his watch and then looks back at* CARMEN. *We hear silence or sound that suggests silence.*

ELLIOT: I'd like it.

CARMEN: No.

ELLIOT: No, I would: I'd like it.

CARMEN gestures at ELLIOT's watch.

CARMEN: How long has—have . . . ?

ELLIOT: *(looking at his watch)* Ten seconds.

Silence.

CARMEN: I said to the secretary: "My husband Elliot Green's a teaching assistant, I'm having a medical emergency, please go get him." She said: "Mr. Green's not married." I said: "Yeah, well, he will be married if I'm having the medical emergency I think I'm having." Then I watched it . . . click, she said: "Just a minute, Mrs. Green." Then I had to wait there, with that . . . information in the . . . *(gestures to the air)* . . . She wanted to know how long we've been together. I said a year, more or less, a year since I fucked you. I didn't say that. It felt mean calling you out of class, but I just—I didn't want to . . . leave you a message on your answering machine, or—

ELLIOT: I'm happy you called me out of class.

Beat.

I love you.

Beat.

I . . . love you—

CARMEN: That's not germane.

Pause as ELLIOT tries to work out how it's not germane.

ELLIOT: What's germane then?

Beat.

I have . . . money for us?

CARMEN: Yeah, that's not—come on.

ELLIOT: "Come on" . . . what . . . ?

CARMEN: There's—!

ELLIOT: What?

CARMEN: There's *grease* that's dripped down the side of your fridge and it's pooled on the floor. There's dust *rolling* down your hallway—

ELLIOT: That's germane?

Pause.

My mom was—I've told you she was hippyish—well, she bought me dolls to play with, I was the only boy in the neighbourhood who played with dolls, and I was good with the dolls, all the family friends said so, I was always washing them and clothing them, taking them for walks in their . . . stroller.

Pause.

I'm conscious my apartment's dirty, in the same way I'm conscious my eyes are bloodshot and my hands are starting to ache—

CARMEN: My dad left my mom by herself with me and my sister—

ELLIOT: Yeah that's not—that's because . . .

Beat: CARMEN *looks at* ELLIOT.

That's because your mother's a monster.

CARMEN: No she's not!

ELLIOT: No: yeah, she's a monster.

CARMEN: She's—no—she's bitter, because she got left with two kids / to raise by herself!

ELLIOT: Last time—last time she called your house, she told me your ex-fiancé's better looking than me.

CARMEN: He is.

ELLIOT: Okay.

CARMEN: He had a bigger cock too.

ELLIOT: Yeah?

CARMEN: Yes.

ELLIOT: How much bigger?

CARMEN: Twice the size of yours.

ELLIOT: *(measuring it out with his hands)* So like that?

CARMEN: *Bigger.*

ELLIOT: So it probably ruptured your cervix . . .

CARMEN: . . . yeah . . .

ELLIOT: . . . when you had sex with him, you had to go to the hospital . . .

CARMEN: . . . mmhm . . .

ELLIOT: . . . and get it stitched up, up there—

CARMEN: I did and I lay there in the hospital moaning in ecstasy.

Silence.

ELLIOT: I'm writing my PhD—

CARMEN: Yeah, well, yesterday, I clipped my toenails. And then I tweezed a couple of hairs out of the mole on my back. And then I worked on my symphony, and that fulfilled me for seven hours, and then I wanted to be fulfilled in another way than work, so I called you and you didn't pick up, so I called *my mother*, and for forty-five minutes she talked about my *sister*, and how my sister bought a house just down the street from her, and how . . . !

Beat.

(calmer) I haven't seen or heard from you in a week. We're in a public washroom, doing a pregnancy test—

ELLIOT: *(low)* I'm sorry.

CARMEN: Yeah?

ELLIOT: I—I'm . . . sorry: I know I'm being . . .

Beat.

I've been trying to get through this . . . part, when I get through it, I'll / slow down.

CARMEN: This part! This part!

ELLIOT: I—yeah: this part.

CARMEN: This part!

ELLIOT: Yeah this part! I've—look, I've *stopped* clipping my toenails. I'm not even ... masturbating. I've only been doing it when I'm so distracted by my crotch that I can't concentrate—!

CARMEN: Do you even *like me?*

ELLIOT: I'm forcing myself to try and get / through this so I can ...

CARMEN: ... *do you / even* ... ?

ELLIOT: ... so I can—yes I like you! I like you and I want to get through this ... *part!*

    Silence.

You don't want it.

CARMEN: No I don't want it!

ELLIOT: Why not?

CARMEN: Because it's *not planned* / and ...

ELLIOT: So?

CARMEN: ... and ...

ELLIOT: So?

CARMEN: ... *and* you're not ready!

ELLIOT: How is it that you ... ! How do you think people have families? They get loaded and they fuck someone they can *barely tolerate.* Then they do it *again.* My parents were *miserable:* they had four kids. Have you seen a birth? I have, I was six: I watched my sister being born. My mother *shit herself.* Then we all had cake. You know what the cake tasted like? Blood. That's how much of it was *in the air.* There was a placenta in the *bathtub.* Then my mother decided she was good to walk around the house—this was one hour after the birth—and you know what happened? She fell down the stairs. It—it's a mess, it's not some planned . . . thing—!

CARMEN: Yeah but, Elliot, I don't want to be like your family or . . . *my / family—*

ELLIOT: Come on, you know what I'm / saying.

CARMEN: You're saying you can't be ready for this, so you're ready, but do you get what I'm saying? Do you get that *I am by myself* most of / the time . . .

ELLIOT: *No, that's not even— / no . . .*

CARMEN: . . . yes it is!

ELLIOT: No, you *like being alone,* / you . . .

CARMEN: . . . no I don't—are you fucking out of your mind!

ELLIOT: *You're a composer! You're a composer!* You work *by yourself—*

CARMEN: Elliot, you have a pathological—

ELLIOT: You know exactly why I . . .

CARMEN: . . . a pathological . . .

ELLIOT: . . . go into my work and don't come out: you're exactly the same!

CARMEN: Yeah but I still know *what a phone is for.* And yeah—I'm single-minded about my work, and it's solitary, which means I don't ask you for much, so why can't you fucking just give me the very / small amount I . . . !

ELLIOT: Okay okay okay but this is my . . . ! You're fine with being alone, you just don't like waiting around for me to call you . . .

CARMEN: . . . no: no . . .

ELLIOT: . . . because it makes you feel like you're this clichéd woman who's at home arranging the flowers . . .

CARMEN: . . . no I am . . .

ELLIOT: . . . while I'm off somewhere banging my secretary . . .

CARMEN: . . . I am *lonely*.

ELLIOT: . . . when this *isn't anything as big as gender politics* it's just *me*, trying to write my PhD!

> *They look at each other, pissed off; they're both breathing a little hard. Then CARMEN looks down at the pregnancy stick.*

What is it?

CARMEN: Two lines.

ELLIOT: So that's a yes.

CARMEN: No it's one line if I am.

ELLIOT: No it's two if you are.

CARMEN: Elliot.

ELLIOT: I'm not kidding.

CARMEN scrabbles around and picks up the instruction form that's lying on the ground. She looks at it.

CARMEN: You're right.

ELLIOT smiles. CARMEN nearly punches him.

ELLIOT: *(flinching)* Don't, don't don't . . . !

CARMEN: Why are you *smiling!!!*

ELLIOT: Because I'm happy!

Long silence as CARMEN considers. Meanwhile, ELLIOT beams.

CARMEN: *(realizing)* You're—you—you're happy?

ELLIOT: I'm happy.

CARMEN: *(sincere)* That's . . . nice.

Beat.

If you leave me alone with this kid, I'll throw it in the garbage.

Transition.

Interlude Act One Scene Four–Five.

Scene Five.

SARAH JEAN speaks to us.

SARAH JEAN: Okay: I'm just going to go through my whole . . . romantic history.

Beat.

When I was in . . . high school, I had a crush on . . . K'an, a guy named K'an. He was very quiet and . . . thoughtful, and I liked that his name had an apostrophe in it: "K" apostrophe, "A," "N." I . . . liked him so much I couldn't talk to him, so instead I made out with his best friend. (The best friend kept talking about his balls, and how his balls were bigger than average, and how his balls hung very low. I kept asking him questions about K'an.) In the end, I didn't even talk to K'an: I just spent a whole lot of time cradling his best friend's balls, and K'an dated one of the exchange students from Iceland.

Beat.

K'an, yeah . . .

Beat.

I dated the guy with big balls for two, two and a half years, before I told him I was only dating him because of my crush on K'an. He was . . . very angry so I tried to explain my thinking to him, which was: he was friends with K'an, he was the same type of guy as K'an, so what difference did it make?

SARAH JEAN considers. Then, a little hostile:

Fine, I see how that sounds, but: what difference *does* it make? It's high school: all the guys are kind of the same guy. No one's got a personality yet.

Transition.

Scene Six.

CARMEN is standing in the front hall, by herself, holding a diaper bag. There is a stroller in front of her that she's gazing into. CARMEN takes a stress breath.

CARMEN goes back to strapping the baby in. Silence. Then ELLIOT enters with a coat on. ELLIOT puts his arms around CARMEN, kisses her.

CARMEN: You were at the office?

ELLIOT: No, a meeting, with a neuroscientist. He said he found my thoughts on time "accessible"—how's Sarah Jean?

CARMEN: Cranky.

ELLIOT: How cranky?

CARMEN: I don't know: cranky.

ELLIOT: *(whispering to the baby)* Buster, Buster, Buster.

CARMEN: She's going to think that's her name.

> *ELLIOT kisses CARMEN, not perfunctory: intimate, sexual.*
>
> *Beat: ELLIOT takes CARMEN in.*

ELLIOT: When you say Sarah Jean's cranky, do you mean you're cranky?

> *Beat.*

Why?

> *Beat.*

Your mom called.

CARMEN: She pruned the pear tree in her backyard by herself. She took out an instructional video from the library, and she pruned it.

> *Beat.*

ELLIOT: Yeah?

CARMEN: That was the part of our conversation that went well. Then I got off the phone, and Sarah Jean cried, and I couldn't get her to stop, so I cried. Then I wrestled her into the stroller as I was crying and she was crying, and that somehow worked and she's fallen asleep, and now I'm just standing here like a zombie.

ELLIOT: It was bad.

CARMEN: It was bad.

> ELLIOT *kisses and holds* CARMEN.

ELLIOT: Does "accessible" sound like a pejorative to you? "Accessible . . . "?

> *Beat:* CARMEN *looks at* ELLIOT. ELLIOT *clocks it.*

Oh, okay, I'm taking about myself, and . . . yeah, okay, I'll—yeah.

> ELLIOT *puts his arms around* CARMEN *and holds her.*
>
> *He hums music from the final scene of the play.*

CARMEN: *(realizing)* That's mine?! That's my piece.

ELLIOT: Mmhm!

CARMEN: You . . . know it?

ELLIOT: I—yeah, I like it?

CARMEN: You *do?*

ELLIOT: I listen to it for hours.

CARMEN: *How?*

ELLIOT: The recording I have of it.

CARMEN: What—when I played it for you? On your Dictaphone?

ELLIOT: Yeah.

CARMEN: Hunh.

ELLIOT: It's haunting.

CARMEN: Yeah it's a little on the tonal side.

ELLIOT: It—no—it helps me to think.

CARMEN: It does?

ELLIOT: Yeah.

They smile. ELLIOT hums the music.

You'd like what I'm doing now: I'm thinking that loop quantum gravity and string theory are different ways of doing *the same thing* and it's all somehow tied together in the deep nature of time: that there's a possible matrix unification of strings and loops. No one's going to agree with me: I mean, it's—that's a very controversial—

CARMEN: Yeah.

ELLIOT: I'm going to bring it up in seminar and watch them lose their fucking minds.

CARMEN: I do like that.

ELLIOT: You do like that.

CARMEN hesitates.

CARMEN: I was thinking . . .

ELLIOT smiles, is about to go through to the kitchen.

Wait, wait . . .

ELLIOT turns back.

You home for . . . You home for lunch?

ELLIOT: Just grabbing a sandwich.

CARMEN: Would you . . . ?

Beat.

We're . . . not spending . . . much time together, and I wanted to know if you'd meet me for lunch once a week.

ELLIOT: Mm?

CARMEN: Would you meet me for lunch, once a / week?

ELLIOT: I'm just home to grab a sandwich?

Beat.

CARMEN: *(suddenly pissed off)* No, I'm asking . . . !

CARMEN's sudden burst of anger means that ELLIOT is paying attention now, looking at CARMEN. CARMEN tries again, calmer this time:

You meet your thesis advisor once a week, for lunch, and I want to come and meet you, have a lunch meeting, once a / week.

ELLIOT: That's for my PhD.

Beat.

CARMEN: On Thursdays, I could come to campus. I'll ask one of the neighbours to take Sarah Jean, I'll come to you, you just have to leave your office for an / hour—

ELLIOT: I'm focusing on finishing my PhD, so it can be finished.

CARMEN: I know—

ELLIOT: That's what we agreed I'd be / doing—

CARMEN: I know, but—

ELLIOT: You said—you said finish your PhD, so you don't get to make me into the big bad—

CARMEN: I know, but—

ELLIOT: The big bad—

CARMEN: I know but when we were coming up with this plan, I didn't realize that when I don't get to see you / I—

ELLIOT: I'm a couple of months away from handing it in—

CARMEN: I know you think that, but—

ELLIOT: I'm working every minute I'm awake to get through / it—

CARMEN: I know! I know you want to finish it—

ELLIOT: *You* want me to finish it!

CARMEN: No, I need us to spend time together because, very soon, I'm going to forget not to fuck other people.

ELLIOT: When's . . .

> *ELLIOT looks at CARMEN and tries to get his temper under control. When he thinks he's calm:*

When's your mother coming?

CARMEN: Why?

ELLIOT: I'll meet you for lunch.

CARMEN: No, why?

ELLIOT: Because she's supposed to get you through this.

CARMEN: If my mother comes she'll make it . . . so much worse, because she'll tell me that you are a shitty, shitty husband, and I'll be like: "I know, Mom, but I agreed—I'm the one that agreed that Elliot could have this time to work." And my mom will be like: "Elliot is a homosexual. I have nothing against homosexuals but do you know how many lives they've wrecked?" And I'll be like: "Mom, we've been over this, he isn't a homosexual, he's a PhD candidate." And then she'll go on and on about my sister, and how my sister is the light of her life, and how my sister's little boys are the light of her life, and how wonderful it is to have grandchildren who live nearby . . .

Beat: CARMEN *tries to not cry.*

ELLIOT: I'll call my mother.

CARMEN: I called your mother.

ELLIOT: And?

CARMEN: Have you met your mother?

Beat.

I called her—she talked about herself—she has a dress she likes that she tore on a lawn mower, so she talked about that for ten minutes. I asked her if you cried a lot as a baby. She said: "Yes." She said she used to stand over your crib and watch you cry. I said: "You didn't . . . ? You didn't pick him up?"

Beat.

Then she told me she'd planned to abort you. But your sisters talked her out of it.

Beat.

Did you know that?

ELLIOT: Yeah.

CARMEN: That's fucked up.

Beat.

Our families are crazy.

Beat.

ELLIOT: And?

CARMEN: And what?

ELLIOT: Is my mother going to come and keep you company?

CARMEN: ARE YOU LISTENING TO ME!

ELLIOT: I WILL MEET YOU FOR LUNCH!

Beat.

I will meet you for lunch.

Transition.

Interlude Act One Scene Six–Seven.

Scene Seven.

SARAH JEAN: My first year at Harvard, I shared a room with . . . my big blond American friend, from Iowa. She was very . . . *(gestures)* . . . outgoing, uninhibited. One time, when I came into our dorm room, she was sleeping face down and naked on her bed. I unlocked the door and I was looking straight into her vagina. It was very large and blond and wrinkled. It had a string hanging out of it.

Beat.

Two days later we were at a party together and she said to me: "If I get so drunk tonight that I can't take my tampon out, will you do it for me?"

Beat.

I said yes.

Beat.

She hugged me and after that, we were best friends, in a lopsided kind of way. She told me over and over again I was her favourite person at college. But the thing is, the only reason I said "yes" about the tampon was because of that split second when I'd opened the door and seen her vagina with a string hanging out of it *and I'd kind of wanted to pull on the string.*

Pause as SARAH JEAN *tries to think about what that means.*

I don't know. That's only marginally related.

Beat.

Isn't it?

Transition.

Interlude Act One Scene Seven–Eight.

Scene Eight.

There is the feeling on stage of being the middle of the night, when suicides peak and the best novels are being written on amphetamines. ELLIOT is working on the floor, papers spread out around him, making notes, searching through piles. There's a manic quality to what ELLIOT's doing. CARMEN enters. She's in a cute little tank top and baggy sweats, and her hair is messy. She's rubbing her eyes. She's holding some old dishes: a glass of wine that's empty, a bowl with scraps and tissues in it, and a spoon. She stands and looks at ELLIOT for a couple of seconds. Finally, ELLIOT senses her there, turns around, and sees her. He tenses for a second, looking at her, then goes back to looking down at and searching through his papers.

ELLIOT: I'm just . . . sorting through these—these old uh . . .

CARMEN comes and perches near ELLIOT.

ELLIOT looks up at her.

. . . uh notes . . . ?

CARMEN: Why?

ELLIOT: . . . I . . . sorry, I uh . . .

Pause.

ELLIOT searches through papers.

Then he remembers that he's talking to CARMEN.

. . . I'm just looking for—I jotted it down, it was something about a contradiction in my work . . .

Silence as CARMEN *continues to watch* ELLIOT.

ELLIOT *continues to go through his piles of papers.*

He looks up again when he realizes that CARMEN *is still there.*

CARMEN: Do you feel good?

ELLIOT: Mm?

CARMEN: Do you feel good?

ELLIOT: Yeah, yeah, I've been thinking a lot about *relief*, as an emotion, it's like this . . . unhinged, dense . . . happiness, and yeah I felt that . . . mmm whenever it was, two weeks ago, after my thesis presentation, but uh . . .

Pause.

ELLIOT *searches through papers.*

(to himself) . . . yeah it . . . *(shakes his head)* . . .

Beat.

CARMEN: So what—what is it, what's the thing that's making you come in here, in the middle of the night, and . . . crouch on the floor, and . . . sift through . . . those piles, what—what's . . . ?

ELLIOT: Mm?

CARMEN: What're you're doing in here in the middle of the night: what are you doing, what's the *thing* you're doing?

Beat.

ELLIOT: Work?

CARMEN: *What work.* What *possible* work can you be doing? *You're finished your fucking work—!*

ELLIOT: You . . . !

Beat.

You were asleep—you were *unconscious!* Why are you / yelling?

CARMEN: WHAT THE FUCK IS WRONG WITH YOU!!!

ELLIOT: What difference can it possibly make to you if I'm down here at FOUR IN THE MORNING, WHAT DO YOU WANT FROM ME, WHAT'S WRONG WITH YOU, why don't we ever talk about what's wrong with you, what do you want: what do you want? You want to tie a rope around / me?

CARMEN: No, shut up.

ELLIOT: No: *what?* We don't say "shut up" to each other?

CARMEN: *Shut up*, you *dick*.

Beat.

(calmer, vocally less intense) What's the thing: what's making you work like this? Why are you like this?

ELLIOT: Like *what?*

Beat.

I'm just—yeah: I'm having a hard time gearing down—listen, no, listen—I know, I know!

CARMEN: No you don't know!

ELLIOT: No, I'm sorry. I'm sorry—

ELLIOT has gone over to CARMEN, closes the distance between them, and goes to kiss her.

CARMEN: No!

ELLIOT goes to kiss her again, more forcefully.

They struggle.

No!

ELLIOT: Let me—

CARMEN: No—

ELLIOT: Let me . . . kiss you—

ELLIOT forces the kiss. CARMEN pushes him off and backs up and looks at him.

Pause.

CARMEN: *(calmly)* I . . . don't want this. I want to watch a little TV, I want to have a little sex, I want to follow a little politics, just enough to vote for the *wrong fucking party*, I want to take my daughter to soccer practice and flute concert, or whatever instrument or sport she likes—

ELLIOT: No you don't.

CARMEN: Yes that is what I want!!!

ELLIOT: You—no! You're a—no.

CARMEN: Elliot, you know what I've called my latest piece? *The Unaccompanied Violin Suites* because it's one violinist . . .

ELLIOT: . . . yeah and . . .

CARMEN: . . . playing by *herself!*

ELLIOT: . . . and you can romanticize being ordinary all you like but the truth is . . .

CARMEN: One lonely violinist!

ELLIOT: . . . you're not ordinary, and you didn't want an ordinary husband so just . . . !

CARMEN: Just . . . what?

ELLIOT: *(new tone)* Let's talk about *you.* Let's talk about your mother. She loves *your sister* more than she loves you. Let's talk about why you think I love my work more than I love you in the context of—

CARMEN: Don't—

ELLIOT: —your fucked-up family—

CARMEN: That's not—that—that's—that's a fucking awful thing to say—she doesn't love my sister more than me—

ELLIOT: Yeah she does.

CARMEN: She wants me to live closer / to her, that's—

ELLIOT: She loves you less. It makes you think *I* love you less but I don't, I . . .

CARMEN: . . . Okay don't . . .

ELLIOT: . . . just came into my office in the middle of the night because *I felt like it*!

CARMEN: Don't wake her up!

> *CARMEN is holding up a hand and listening intently, tensely. We hear a far-off sound that might be a baby. Then silence.*

I thought I heard her . . .

> *CARMEN listens.*

> *But the house is quiet now.*

> *Pause.*

ELLIOT: Listen, I'll stop now, I'm finished my . . . PhD—and I will . . . stop now, I said I would and I . . . meant it when I said it.

CARMEN: Yeah?

ELLIOT: Yeah.

> *Beat.*

CARMEN: *Can* you stop?

ELLIOT: Yes.

CARMEN: Can you?

> *Silence as ELLIOT considers the question.*

Can you?

ELLIOT: *(shrugs)* Maybe . . . maybe . . . look, maybe . . . ? I don't know—I don't know: yeah, I . . . don't know. I like to work, it yeah—it gives me something—I have this sense that I can contribute something that's . . . substantial and I want to—I don't know, sometimes, it almost surfaces. And my PhD was . . . I did feel relief, and I . . . know the department was . . . happy with it, but I don't think I went far enough with it—

CARMEN: You unified string theory and loop quantum gravity / using—

ELLIOT: I—yes—I know, fine, good, yes, but it's limited. Like I can't broaden my . . . I have this sense that it's just out of reach, I don't know, it's . . . bothering me, it's . . . and I feel like if I keep going, I'll get there.

    Beat.

And that thought, it's . . . not leaving me alone.

    Beat.

(hesitating) Yeah . . .

    Beat.

I—yeah—if I'm being—if I'm being . . . very—I *do* still have something to . . . prove.

    Pause.

CARMEN: Elliot?

ELLIOT: Yeah?

CARMEN: You know that when I talk to the secretary of the Harvard physics department she tells me that they've never had a PhD candidate who's as talented as you in the whole time she's been the secretary—which is thirty-seven years.

Beat.

Did you know that?

ELLIOT nods.

It . . . doesn't make it . . . better?

ELLIOT shakes his head.

ELLIOT: No.

CARMEN: No, hunh.

Beat.

Do you think it's because your mother didn't want you.

Beat.

ELLIOT: *(low)* Maybe.

Silence.

CARMEN: Do you think I should leave you?

Beat.

ELLIOT: Yeah.

CARMEN: Yeah?

ELLIOT: *(very low)* You're not happy.

Beat.

CARMEN: There's a house down the street that's for rent. On the south side: it had a rent sign on it so I went and looked at it . . .

ELLIOT: When did you . . . ?

CARMEN shrugs.

CARMEN: Monday?

Beat.

ELLIOT: Is it nice?

CARMEN: Yeah, it is nice.

ELLIOT: The narrow one?

CARMEN: Yeah.

ELLIOT: The roof looks a little run down, but that could be fixed.

Silence as CARMEN and ELLIOT look at each other. Then ELLIOT turns back to his work, his papers. ELLIOT works. CARMEN stands there, struggles with herself, and then, finally, she starts to break down and cry. She puts her hands over her face:

CARMEN: *(low, beaten)* Don't you . . . love me?

ELLIOT turns and looks at her.

Don't you even love me a little?

ELLIOT: I love you, I—of course I love you: I love you so much, but is that germane . . . ?

CARMEN goes to ELLIOT and holds him.

Of course I love you.

CARMEN: Yeah?

ELLIOT: How can you think I don't love you?

CARMEN: Yeah?

ELLIOT: I love you so much: I love you . . . so much, so much . . . *(repeat at the actor's discretion)* . . .

> *Then ELLIOT is gathering CARMEN up and kissing her, a little as though he's giving her CPR, breathing life back into her. The transition here is larger; it suggests a larger durational change, the passage of more time than all the past transitions.*

Music For Life.

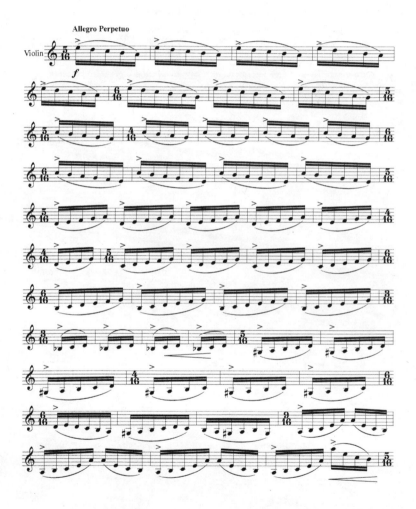

By the end of the music, SARAH JEAN *will arrive in the story of her parents.* CARMEN *and* ELLIOT *will kiss and hold each other.* SARAH JEAN *will force her way between them.*

Throughout the music we hear SARAH JEAN *speaking little words in a toddler's voice, a two-year-old's voice:*

SARAH JEAN: Miwk! Miwk! Mmmmmmuuuuuhhhh! Miwk!

Then SARAH JEAN progresses to little phrases in a four-year-old's voice:

Mommy, mm, where's my milk, I can't find it, it's . . . oh it's right here! *(giggling)* It's right here! It was here all along on the table the whole time, Mommy!

Then SARAH JEAN progresses to longer phrases in a seven-year-old's voice:

Oh no, Mom: oh come in here, please! There's an . . . emergency, I spilled milk on my . . . music, oh no I need a little cloth, can you bring it, it's going everywhere into the cracks in the floor and it's on the . . . bottom of my shoes! Ah! Ahhhhh! Mom!!!

SARAH JEAN *dissolves into giggles.*

Transition.

Scene Nine.

SARAH JEAN: When I was in my . . . final year of college, I gave a hand job to a guy I didn't like very much. I just got so lonely.

Beat.

My big blond American friend had transferred to a public university in Wisconsin because her grades weren't high enough, and my mathematics professor had ended our affair when his wife found out about it. So I went to a film noir appreciation club and this . . . person kept talking to me so I gave him a hand job. He was the type of guy who'd put tick marks in a volume of Kafka when he approved of the turn of phrase.

Beat.

After that, I was his girlfriend for . . . nine months, because . . . he kept saying he was horribly in love with me and then he . . . started moving his things into my apartment . . . ?

Beat.

Then one evening we went to the symphony, and he held the program in one hand and a pen in the other, and after each movement he crossed it out in the program.

Beat.

Later that night I picked a fight with him. We were at my apartment and I was making him dinner, and sometimes when I make dinner for men I feel resentment irrationally rising in me. I told him it was terrible when he talked about how haunting the sound of the female orgasm is because *how would he know?*

Beat.

He looked . . . stunned and he said he thought he gave me lots of orgasms. I said: "Fine, fine that's true, but they're not *haunting*."

Beat.

I said it was disgusting he pretended he didn't watch pornography. It didn't make it any better that he watched vintage pornography from the seventies, with all the pubic hair. It wasn't a highbrow hobby: it was pornography. I mean, he jerked off to it. Was he jerking off ironically?

Beat.

He started ripping a hole in my sofa. Then he put his head down and cried. He said he was sorry, a couple of times.

Beat.

I couldn't stop—I couldn't . . . stop: he was face down in the sofa and I said: "Music is my solace!" But I yelled it, like, "MUSIC IS MY SOLACE!!!" Which is a dumb, incomprehensible thing to yell at someone.

Beat.

When he stopped . . . crying, he said he'd send a friend for his things.

Beat.

He crept out: he . . . crept out.

Beat.

So, yeah, I guess that was a little . . . cold of me. Yeah. But he was only crying like that because I made him feel like a loser. It wasn't *heartbreak*.

Beat.

It wasn't.

Transition.

SARAH JEAN *goes and picks up her violin . . .*

Scene Ten.

SARAH JEAN *is staring at an electric alarm clock, one of those old ones with big bold white numerals that click over. The clock reads 6:44 a.m.* SARAH JEAN *is holding her violin and her bow's poised in the air, ready to play, but she's waiting. After at least twenty seconds the clock stutters a little—tries to click over—and then it clicks over to 6:45 a.m., and* SARAH JEAN *starts playing the violin.*

Tantrum.

She's playing it furiously, loudly, and at a frenetic pace. She's throwing a sort of musical tantrum. After twenty seconds to a minute of horrible sound ELLIOT *stumbles in, in a shirt and boxers or pyjamas: he's in the clothes that he sleeps in.*

ELLIOT: Buster! Buster! No, come on: what's happening?

ELLIOT snatches the bow out of SARAH JEAN's *hands.* SARAH JEAN *starts jumping and grabbing at it to try and get it back from* ELLIOT.

SARAH JEAN: Give it to me! Give me my . . . bow . . . ! I'm practising! I'm practising: *this is my practice time!!!*

ELLIOT: This is not your practice time.

SARAH JEAN: *Yeah it is!*

ELLIOT holds the bow even higher. It's well out of her reach. ELLIOT *and* CARMEN *stare at each other, panting.*

ELLIOT: It's 6:45 a.m.

SARAH JEAN: I know it's 6:45 a.m.! Mom said I could start practising at 6:45 a.m.!

ELLIOT: That can't be true.

SARAH JEAN: It is true—!!!

ELLIOT: No, I'm not giving you back the bow: you're going to snap it—

SARAH JEAN: *(jumping for it again)* I *want* to snap it!

ELLIOT: *No!*

SARAH JEAN: *I want to snap it uuuhhhhhhhhhrrrraaaaaahhhhhhh!*

SARAH JEAN struggles with him again. When she fails to get her bow back, she throws herself onto the floor.

ELLIOT: Sarah Jean—

SARAH JEAN: *Fuck off!*

ELLIOT: *Whoa!!!*

SARAH JEAN is sobbing on the ground. ELLIOT looks at her for a second, and then:

(calling) Carmen!

SARAH JEAN: *(muffled)* She can fuck off too!

ELLIOT: Okay, Buster, this is . . . ! What's happening?

SARAH's tantrum worsens.

Please don't swear like that.

SARAH JEAN: *(muffled by the tantrum)* You swear!

ELLIOT: I swear in lectures—

SARAH JEAN: *Uuuhhhhhhhhhrrrraaaaaahhhhhhh!*

Beat. SARAH JEAN stares at ELLIOT: WAITING FOR A RESPONSE.

ELLIOT: I swear in lectures because it's funny when scientists swear, and I'm trying to introduce a little humour into theoretical physics.

And the momentary lull in SARAH JEAN's tantrum is over. SARAH JEAN responds to ELLIOT with an even bigger tantrum. ELLIOT looks down at her for a few more seconds.

(to himself, as SARAH JEAN freaks out) Okay.

ELLIOT picks up a piece of paper and a pencil off the ground, and then he draws on the paper. SARAH JEAN's tantrum winds down. She sits up, wipes her face, and looks at what ELLIOT's doing. SARAH JEAN hyperventilates as she talks.

SARAH JEAN: Y . . . you're . . . you're drawing?

ELLIOT: Yeah.

SARAH JEAN: Wh . . . wh . . . ?

ELLIOT: What am I drawing?

SARAH JEAN: Y . . . yeah.

ELLIOT: Time.

SARAH JEAN: Why?

ELLIOT: Tell me, Buster: is time a road, or a hospital, or a prison?

SARAH JEAN: Mm.

ELLIOT: Mm?

SARAH JEAN: It's a w . . . war.

ELLIOT: Yeah? Why?

SARAH JEAN: I don't know.

ELLIOT: Yeah, and what does it sound like?

Beat. Then as ELLIOT draws:

If I listen very closely, I hear it.

SARAH JEAN: Yeah?

ELLIOT: Mmmhmm, yeah.

Beat.

For a long time it was . . . very faint.

SARAH JEAN: Yeah?

ELLIOT: Yeah, and it sounded . . . like students, pushing back their chairs . . .

ELLIOT touches a hand to his forehead: pain.

. . . and like a little girl counting backwards from ten . . .

SARAH JEAN: Yeah?

ELLIOT: But then I met your mom, and I could hear it clearly for the first time. It was your mom whispering my name over and over and over—Elliot, Elliot, Elliot—like that, and it—it was the most beautiful—the most beautiful sound.

Beat.

Do you think time has a sound?

SARAH JEAN: Mm . . .

ELLIOT: Can you hear it?

SARAH JEAN: Mm. Sometimes.

ELLIOT: And what does it sound like to you?

SARAH JEAN: *(shy)* Mmmmmm . . .

ELLIOT: Most people think time sounds like a clock.

ELLIOT realizes.

Oh *shit*, oh crap, I'm sorry—

SARAH JEAN: You were supposed to get me a new alarm clock. And Mom won't get me a new alarm clock because you're supposed to do it. And I have a *very crappy* alarm clock, Dad. It's broken: it doesn't go off. So I got up late. It's six forty-eight and I haven't had my shower, I haven't had my breakfast, I won't have time to practise . . . *(hyperventilates)* . . .

Beat.

(very sincerely upset) I can't . . . g . . . get the morning back . . . *(hyperventilates)* . . .

ELLIOT: No, you can't.

Beat.

You know you're eight years old, right?

SARAH JEAN: Yeah I know I'm eight years old!

ELLIOT: Okay, okay, you know that time's a construct? It's made up?

SARAH JEAN: *What are you even talking about?!*

ELLIOT: I'm saying, don't get upset about time, because it's . . . fake. The universe is timeless, and there are timeless laws. Time itself doesn't have substance. When you're older you'll read Newton and Einstein and you'll see it's like religion: it's just a dumb story that got repeated too much.

Pause: SARAH JEAN stares at ELLIOT.

SARAH JEAN: *(low)* You are making me very angry.

ELLIOT: Okay, Buster, I'm sorry, let me give you the schedule, you and Mom are coming to the keynote lecture I'm giving today at the University of Toronto, do you remember that—

SARAH JEAN: *Uuuhhhhhhhhhrrrraaaaaahhhhhhh then* . . . then *when* are you getting me the clock?!!!!!

CARMEN *enters.*

SARAH JEAN *looks at* CARMEN *and then moves to the door.*

CARMEN: *(to* SARAH JEAN, *as she's exiting)* Honey . . .

SARAH JEAN storms out.

CARMEN and ELLIOT look at each other.

ELLIOT makes a not totally sincere "I give up," "I have no idea what that was about" hand gesture—he's lying to cover his ass.

ELLIOT: I . . . don't know . . . !

Beat.

CARMEN comes over and holds him.

CARMEN: I think she's still upset you forgot her at school.

ELLIOT: I'm a . . .

ELLIOT touches a hand to his forehead: pain.

I'm a shitty father?

Beat.

I'm a shitty father, is that the . . . ? Is that where this is going, because let's just get to it.

CARMEN: You're a good father who occasionally forgets to pick his daughter up from school—

ELLIOT: I'm a shitty father.

CARMEN: *(smiling)* You're a somewhat shitty father, but you have other qualities. You're also "a mediocre scientist . . . "

ELLIOT: Ha ha.

CARMEN: " . . . who, despite potential, has failed to make a significant contribution to his chosen field."

ELLIOT: *(sincerely searching)* Are you quoting . . . something . . . ?

CARMEN: Yeah: you.

ELLIOT: I said that?

CARMEN: Yeah.

> *ELLIOT lifts a hand to his forehead again: pain.*

(kind) You okay?

ELLIOT: I—my head aches.

CARMEN: She *was* yelling very loudly.

> *ELLIOT and CARMEN smile a little.*

> *SARAH JEAN comes in.*

SJ, I'm going to take you to get the clock after the lecture.

SARAH JEAN: Okay but how long from now?

ELLIOT: When you've counted to . . . Twenty-seven thousand eight hundred and forty-two seconds, that's when we'll be going, okay, Buster?

> *ELLIOT kisses her. ELLIOT starts exiting as she starts counting.*

SARAH JEAN: One, two, three, four, five, six, seven, eight, nine, ten, eleven, twelve, thirteen, fourteen, fifteen, sixteen—

ELLIOT: *(over his shoulder)* You should count down.

SARAH JEAN: Hunh?

ELLIOT: Count. Down.

SARAH JEAN: Twenty-seven thousand eight hundred and forty two, twenty-seven thousand eight hundred and forty-one, twenty-seven thousand . . .

SARAH JEAN keeps counting under her breath.

ELLIOT exits.

CARMEN goes over to SARAH JEAN and brushes her hair out of her face.

CARMEN: Don't count on it though, okay, honey?

SARAH JEAN: Is that a pun?

CARMEN: Oh.

SARAH JEAN: Is it?

CARMEN: Uh . . . ?

SARAH JEAN: A pun on "count"?

CARMEN: Yeah . . . ?

SARAH JEAN: You roll your eyes when Dad makes puns. You roll your eyes and you say he makes bad jokes, and you roll your eyes at him like this . . .

SARAH JEAN rolls her eyes.

CARMEN: Honey, I'm sorry about all this.

CARMEN reaches out to touch SARAH JEAN's cheek and she flinches away.

I could put on some music for you. Would that help you feel a little better—?

SARAH JEAN: Shhhh! Sh!

Beat.

If you talk I'll lose count.

CARMEN shoots SARAH JEAN a look.

CARMEN: Okay . . . !

CARMEN goes out.

SARAH JEAN: *(half under her breath)* Twenty-seven thousand eight hundred and thirty-five, twenty-seven thousand eight hundred and thirty-four . . . *(mouthing)* . . . twenty-seven thousand eight hundred and . . . *(mouthing)* . . . twenty-seven thousand eight hundred and thirty-one, twenty-seven thousand . . .

Movement. The family enacts a complex and frenetic pattern of relationship. At the end of this, ELLIOT is standing alone, facing the audience.

Transition.

Dance.

Scene Eleven.

We're in a darkened auditorium.

SARAH JEAN and CARMEN sit in the audience.

We focus on ELLIOT, who addresses the audience as at a lecture.

ELLIOT: I'm Elliot Green, I'm a theoretical physicist, and I wrote a book about the history of timekeeping. I got a little stuck with my work . . . about seven, eight years ago, after I finished my PhD, and I started to get bummed out, so I wrote this book as a distraction, and it got on a bestseller list, and now it's proving to be an even bigger distraction.

Pause as ELLIOT looks down at his notes.

He rearranges them a little.

I want to open with an anecdote from the book. It's from the chapter called "Clock-Wars or Who Has the Biggest Clock?" This is from the period in timekeeping history when the Catholic countries of Europe unilaterally adopted a new timekeeping technology, the Gregorian calendar, our current calendar. This was in 1582, and what happened was: Britain held out. For a hundred and seventy years. Because no one—no one—tells the British what time it is. So for a hundred and seventy years the two calendars got more and more out of sync: by 1751, Britain was eleven days behind the continent, which is to say, if you'd crossed the channel on December 11, 1751, you would've arrived in France on December 22.*

Beat.

---

* In production, replace the day and month in the text with the day and month of the performance (and then count eleven days forward for the second date).

A British nobleman named Lord Chesterfield lobbied the House of Lords to reform the calendar. He wasn't a mathematician or an astronomer, but he did have a delightful French mistress living across the channel, and so he became keenly aware of the problem of an eleven-day time difference between England and Europe. What we can determine from this is that the desire for sexual relations, for . . . love, is a determining force in the history of time.

> ELLIOT *looks at* CARMEN *in the audience.*

You probably came here to . . . get a little better informed, but you're very likely going to spend a portion of your time with me thinking about someone you find sexually interesting.

> Beat.

If that "someone" is here with you in the auditorium, like mine is, my wife is here, in the front row . . . Lean over and say softly into their ear: "I want to have intercourse with you more than once." Too scientific? What about: "I would change time for you."

> ELLIOT *smiles at* CARMEN.

(to CARMEN, *low)* I would.

> ELLIOT *smiles at her.*

> *Then he touches his forehead.*

Okay, enough of that, what I want to . . .

> Beat.

What I want to discuss is the . . .

> ELLIOT *touches his forehead.*

... the ... the timeless nature of ... the universe and why it is that scientists understand that time is an illusion ... when most people continue to ... think of time as ... when they, say ... lose eleven days, they ...

ELLIOT touches his forehead.

Pause.

I'm sorry, I ...

CARMEN stands up.

I ...

ELLIOT falls to the ground.

CARMEN: Elliot! Elliot ... !

CARMEN runs onto the stage and kneels over him. ELLIOT is having a seizure. His body spasms. SARAH JEAN has stayed in her seat, paralyzed.

SARAH JEAN: Daddy ... ?

We hear the sound of people pushing back their chairs, a commotion, and the sound of a microphone being knocked off its stand, distant yells ...

Blackout.

In the darkness ...

Ten, nine, eight, seven, six, five, four, three, two ...

Transition.

Intermezzo.

* If less music is needed, cut m. 41-48.

Act Two.
Scene One.

This is a hospital room. There is a hospital bed and ELLIOT *is wearing a hospital gown. There is the buzz and glare of hospital lighting and equipment.* CARMEN *is sitting in a plastic chair beside the hospital bed.* SARAH JEAN *enters.*

SARAH JEAN: *(to CARMEN)* Mom, in the bathroom a girl came out of one of the stalls and she had teeth missing and just . . . blood in her mouth, and the nurse had towels up on the mirrors so she couldn't see her face, and I was asking what happened to her and . . .

CARMEN: . . . come sit for a sec . . .

SARAH JEAN: . . . and the nurse was saying to me "go out" and then she said to the girl "he's not worth it" and I don't know what happened to her?

ELLIOT: Come sit.

SARAH JEAN: What happened to her?

CARMEN: Come sit.

SARAH JEAN: What happened to her, though?

CARMEN: Your dad and I wanted to tell you something, remember we said . . . ?

SARAH JEAN: Yeah?

Beat.

Yeah?

CARMEN: You know how Dad's been in hospital this week . . . ?

Beat.

ELLIOT: I have brain cancer. That's why I . . . had the seizure when I was in the middle of the lecture, and that's why I've been in hospital.

CARMEN: I don't know if you've ever heard much about cancer . . . ? It's a sickness, it's called cancer, like a . . . cold or a flu, but the type of cancer that your dad's been diagnosed with, it . . .

Beat.

ELLIOT: It kills you.

Beat.

Do you understand "kills you"? From what we've read, in your age range, you might not understand that. What it means, in very simple terms, is that, in one to two months from now, I won't be able to . . .

ELLIOT clears his throat, fights a wave of emotion.

I won't be able to see you . . .

Beat.

And, Sarah Jean, Buster, you won't be able to see me either.

SARAH JEAN: *(holding her shirt away from her)* I got some drops of blood! Mom! It's got little drops on it—

CARMEN: I see that.

SARAH JEAN: I want to take it off.

CARMEN: Not yet.

SARAH JEAN: No but I want to take it off.

CARMEN: Did you hear what Dad said?

ELLIOT: Buster, did you hear what I said?

SARAH JEAN: *(to CARMEN)* Please!

CARMEN: Did you hear Dad?

> Beat.

SARAH JEAN: *(shy)* Well don't worry about it, Dad.

> *SARAH JEAN touches ELLIOT's arm lightly, reassuringly.*

Don't worry—don't worry . . . !

> Beat.

ELLIOT: Do you understand what—what we're saying, SJ?

SARAH JEAN: *(to CARMEN)* Can I have a pop. Can I have a pop from the vending machine?

ELLIOT: She can't have a pop.

SARAH JEAN: Can I have a juice from the vending machine?

> *CARMEN takes out some change and gives it to SARAH JEAN. SARAH JEAN goes out and watches the scene from off.*

CARMEN: She took it in.

ELLIOT looks at CARMEN.

ELLIOT: She did?

CARMEN: She's doing what you do. She's going to go think about it, by herself, and then she'll come back and she'll have questions.

Beat.

ELLIOT: *(an understatement)* That was hard.

CARMEN goes over and strokes his hand or hair.

Beat.

When you were pregnant—do you remember this? Our joke was that our kid would turn out to be stupid.

CARMEN: Yeah.

Beat.

The ultrasound technician didn't think it was very funny.

Beat.

She's a lot like you.

ELLIOT: She's a lot like you. She's got your talent with string instruments and mine with string theory, and that's my terrible joke for the day.

Beat.

She twitches her fingers like you do, have you noticed that?

CARMEN: *(low)* Yeah.

> *Beat.*

ELLIOT: Is my mother here yet?

> *Beat.*

No?

CARMEN: No.

> *Beat.*

(low) I'm sorry.

> *Beat.*

Is there anyone else you want to have here who I should call . . . ?

ELLIOT: Uh. Uh . . .

> *Beat.*

My . . . sisters, uh . . . ?

> *Beat.*

CARMEN: Yeah.

> *Beat.*

It's—this is . . . hard.

> *Beat.*

Is there anything you want to . . . do, in the next few weeks . . . ? Is there anything . . . you want to talk about . . . ?

Beat.

ELLIOT: I think . . .

Beat.

It's funny: I think . . . there might be some things about time that I didn't . . . fully . . . get.

Beat.

CARMEN: Yeah?

ELLIOT: Yeah: a few things . . . are . . . hitting me, I think this is going to sound so . . . stupid, when I say it, but . . . I think . . . what if . . . time is not a construct, what if it's . . . real.

CARMEN: Yeah?

ELLIOT: Yeah.

CARMEN: Yeah, it is real.

ELLIOT: No, I mean, I think I . . . disagree with Einstein. I think the old physics might be . . . wrong: maybe time's not mathematical and *there is no formula of everything* that exists outside of . . . time—I think it's that the—the—my twister foam theory contains a contradiction with respect to how I'm representing the nature of time. The theory has two . . . dual . . . When I study the bulk in the loop representation the theory is timeless. But when I go to the boundary theory, time . . . reappears. And I think that the . . . contradiction inherent in the duality can only be . . . resolved by declaring time to be really . . . real. The past corresponds to the timeless loop side of the duality, the future to the time-bound quantum-string-theory side. The past . . . is timeless because it's already happened and so it's fixed. But the future is not timeless: it's open, and uncertain.

CARMEN: Yeah.

ELLIOT: Which means the universe isn't fixed: change is possible.

CARMEN: Yeah it is.

ELLIOT: I—yeah—I just—yeah—I think I've . . . finally uh—finally . . . worked it out: I want to jot down some notes—I want my laptop.

Beat.

CARMEN: You . . . ?

ELLIOT: I'd like my laptop.

CARMEN: You want your laptop. Do you—do you—*really? Really?*

ELLIOT: Yeah?

CARMEN: Do you . . . get that you're dying . . . at all . . . ?

Beat.

ELLIOT: Yeah, I get that—

CARMEN: Dying: you will be dead, like you will be . . . dead, like this is it, this is your last chance: your daughter's going to grow up without you.

ELLIOT: I just said that to her: I just said we don't have much / time!

CARMEN: This is it for her!

ELLIOT: No, you know what—?

CARMEN: —her relationship with her father is coming to a close—!

ELLIOT: I have loved her with *all my heart, and I have loved you with all my heart*—

CARMEN: That's a *crock of shit*—!

Simultaneous text:

ELLIOT: That is not a crock of shit!

CARMEN: You are dying—you are dying—you are dying . . . !

SARAH JEAN is standing in the doorway. She drops her can of soda pop. It spills on the floor. SARAH JEAN's face contorts into a grimace, her knees bend together, she brings her hands up to her face, and she starts to cry.

Transition.

Music For Death.

Scene Two.

SARAH JEAN regards the audience. She's still upset.

SARAH JEAN: The . . . boy I had a crush on in high school—K'an—wrote to me on social media about a year ago. He'd heard through a friend—the friend with big balls—that I was in Montreal.

Beat.

K'an . . . grew up handsome.

SARAH JEAN *smiles.*

K'an's . . . very tall and . . . good in bed—we've been uh . . . dating, because turns out he had a crush on me too!

SARAH JEAN *smiles.*

Yeah! Nice, hunh!

K'an asked me recently why I like him. I said: "I think it's because you used to blush whenever anyone said anything suggestive. So when, say, the gym teacher was putting a condom on a banana, I'd look at you to see if you were going red, and, somehow, getting a sexual feeling and looking at you got mixed up together."

Beat.

Turns out that's not what he wanted to hear.

Beat.

Right around then my mathematics professor called me. I'd asked him to write a reference letter for me, for my PhD application: and so of course I wanted to talk about . . . my PhD application, but he wanted to go on and on about how his most persistent regret is me, and how I'm the love of his life. I told him that was bullshit, and then he cried and said he knew it sounded like bullshit but it wasn't, I wasn't just a sexy student, I had a brain like my dad's. Then I said: will you write the reference letter or not? Then he hung up on me. The upshot is: I told all of that to K'an and K'an . . . got a worried look on his face.

Beat.

But come on, "love of his life"! That *does* sound like bullshit, doesn't it?

Beat.

(very low) Fuck.

Beat.

Then she leans her head against the wall. Then she slumps against it.

Transition.

Interlude Act Two Scene Two–Three.

Scene Three.

CARMEN and SARAH JEAN sit on plastic hospital chairs, waiting. After a silence, during which CARMEN keeps shaking her head:

CARMEN: *(to SARAH JEAN)* I've set you a bad example, honey, a very bad . . . !

Pause.

(to SARAH JEAN) I rented a house down the street from us one time, because I was trying to leave your father, but I—for some reason I didn't and I'm sorry, I'm sorry I paid rent on that house for six months: I want you to know I feel badly about myself all the time because I haven't left him.

SARAH JEAN: It's okay—

CARMEN: No it's not!

SARAH JEAN: But it's okay—

CARMEN: *(to herself)* I don't—I don't—I can't understand why I—I had a good track record of leaving men who disappointed me.

SARAH JEAN: Can I have a pop?

Beat.

Can I have a pop—?

CARMEN: Yeah, yeah.

CARMEN digs in her purse for change for a pop.

He's—he's typing—he's typing in there!

SARAH JEAN: Yeah he is.

CARMEN: He's . . . typing!

SARAH JEAN: Yeah.

CARMEN: We're sitting . . . outside his hospital room and he's typing!

Beat.

What—what . . . ?

Beat.

What's wrong with me? Why didn't I leave that person?

CARMEN tries not to cry.

SARAH JEAN: Mom? Do you know what? He's listening to your violin suite on his headphones.

Beat.

Mom?

CARMEN: Yeah?

SARAH JEAN: That's . . . nice, hunh?

CARMEN: *(sincere, pulling herself together)* Yeah. Yeah, that's nice.

SARAH JEAN: Yeah!

CARMEN and SARAH JEAN both try not to cry.

Transition.

Interlude Act Two Scene Three–Four.

Scene Four.

SARAH JEAN speaks to the audience.

SARAH JEAN: Okay . . . ? Okay . . . ? Here's one.

Beat.

Two . . .

Pause as SARAH JEAN takes a breath, steadies herself.

Two . . . weeks ago, I told K'an: "I'm leaving Montreal, I'm moving to Stanford to do a PhD in mathematics, and so probably our relationship should end."

Beat.

His face went all red.

Beat.

He got out of bed, and put his clothes on, and his sneakers on, and I just . . . watched him.

Beat.

Finally he said: "You've figured out that I love you, right?"

Beat.

I said: "That's just what you're calling the emotion you're feeling because you're not getting what you want."

Beat.

Then he . . . left.

Beat.

I got on the phone with my big blond American friend, and I asked her what was happening and she said: "When guys—when anyone tells you they love you, you don't listen, you don't think it's real, you don't think it means anything, I don't know why: probably because you're fucked up."

Beat.

Yep, that's . . . what she uh . . .

Beat.

I told her she was a fucking American and *what did she know?*

Transition.

Interlude Act Two Scene Four–Five.

Scene Five.

We see ELLIOT, CARMEN, and SARAH JEAN.

ELLIOT has tubes coming out of his nose.

He has a laptop beside him.

CARMEN: *(to SARAH JEAN)* It's okay, go ahead, you can talk to him.

SARAH JEAN: Dad?

ELLIOT: *(low)* Yeah?

SARAH JEAN: Dad?

ELLIOT: *(low)* Yeah?

SARAH JEAN: I can't hear you.

ELLIOT pulls himself up.

He clears his throat a little.

ELLIOT: I'm sorry.

SARAH JEAN: What's going to happen?

ELLIOT: I'm going to eat some cherry-flavoured Jell-O.

SARAH JEAN: And then?

ELLIOT: I'm going to lie here and fall in and out of consciousness.

SARAH JEAN: And then?

ELLIOT: I'll take some pills and talk to some doctors.

SARAH JEAN: And then?

ELLIOT: I'm going to kiss you and Mom.

SARAH JEAN: And then?

ELLIOT: I'm going to say goodbye.

SARAH JEAN: And then?

ELLIOT: I'm going to stop breathing and my limbs'll stiffen.

SARAH JEAN: And then the worms.

ELLIOT: That's right.

Beat.

SARAH JEAN: Will I be able to see you.

ELLIOT: No.

SARAH JEAN: Why?

ELLIOT: Because I'll be buried in a box under the ground.

SARAH JEAN: For how long?

ELLIOT: How long will it take to bury the box?

SARAH JEAN: Uh.

ELLIOT: It takes about an hour. The hole the box is put into is six-feet deep, traditionally, but I don't know if that's still . . . ? Carmen?

CARMEN: Yeah?

ELLIOT: Is the hole going to be six feet deep?

CARMEN: Yeah.

ELLIOT: Why is that?

CARMEN: So wild animals can't dig up the body.

ELLIOT: So, Buster, the gravediggers dig a hole, they put the box in the hole, then they cover the box with the dirt they displaced to dig the hole.

SARAH JEAN: When will I see you?

ELLIOT: You won't see me, Buster, because I'll be in the box.

SARAH JEAN: For how long.

ELLIOT: Infinity. Or in theology: eternity.

   Beat.

People die, Buster.

CARMEN: Honey, Dad needs some water. Could you go ask one of the nurses in the hallway for him?

SARAH JEAN: Can I get a pop now?

CARMEN: Yeah.

   SARAH JEAN goes out.

   ELLIOT puts a hand over his face.

She's drinking pop. I can't say no to her right now.

> *Beat.*

Elliot?

ELLIOT: My . . . legs are cold: I think I'm losing circulation to them. There's pressure behind my eye, it feels like my eye might get pushed out of its socket.

> *Beat.*

I think I'm uh . . . I'm going to . . . go, soon . . .

CARMEN: *(low)* Yeah.

> *Beat.*

Click for some morphine.

> *ELLIOT clicks.*

> *Silence.*

ELLIOT: I'm sorry for—for the ways I've disappointed you . . .

CARMEN: Yeah—?

ELLIOT: I hope . . .

> *Beat.*

CARMEN: You hope what?

> *Pause as* ELLIOT *shakes his head, and then he puts a limp hand on his laptop.*

ELLIOT: Give it to my publisher.

Beat.

It's finished.

Beat.

I've dedicated it to my mother.

ELLIOT slowly, painfully, pushes his laptop towards CARMEN.

ELLIOT lies there and closes his eyes.

CARMEN sits there.

Transition.

Interlude Act Two Scene Five–Six.

Scene Six.

SARAH JEAN speaks to the audience.

SARAH JEAN: K'an came back a couple of hours later, and he said in a very angry tone that he wants to marry me.

Beat.

And then the phone rang and K'an said: "Answer it, it might be Stanford, or, even better, that prof you fucked."

Beat.

But it wasn't, it was an officer from the Toronto Police Service, and he asked if my mother was named Carmen Green, and I said yes, and he asked me if I was by myself, and I said no, and he told me to sit down.

Beat.

I said to K'an: "The police are telling me to sit down," and K'an, he . . . had this look on his face, when he realized what was happening, that was so . . .

Beat.

Haunting.

Beat.

I got off the phone, and he packed me a suitcase, and booked me a flight online.

He said: "I want to marry you" again at the airport when he dropped me off. But it . . . sounded less angry that time, more . . . resigned.

Beat.

Yeah.

Transition.

Interlude Act Two Scene Six–Seven.

Scene Seven.

SARAH JEAN is standing still and listening intently. CARMEN is dressed in formal black.

CARMEN: Did you hear that lady who was crying: I kept looking over to see what was happening, she was standing over a grave the whole service, and just . . . bawling: it was very grating—she kept stopping and starting, stopping and starting—

SARAH JEAN: I think she was sad.

Silence.

SARAH JEAN is listening.

CARMEN looks at SARAH JEAN.

CARMEN: *(to SARAH JEAN)* What are you doing?

SARAH JEAN: Listening.

CARMEN: To what?

SARAH JEAN: Time.

Beat as SARAH JEAN *and* CARMEN *listen.*

I can hear it.

Beat. Off CARMEN's *look:*

I can hear it, Mom?

CARMEN: Okay, honey.

SARAH JEAN: I can hear it.

CARMEN: Yeah?

SARAH JEAN: Yes! Yes I can hear it!?

CARMEN: *(impatient)* How does it sound?

SARAH JEAN: It's like . . . ?

CARMEN: *(impatient)* Like a vacuum cleaner?

SARAH JEAN: No.

CARMEN: *(impatient)* Like a mosquito?

SARAH JEAN: No.

CARMEN: *(impatient)* Like a . . . harp?

SARAH JEAN: No? No, more like a person.

CARMEN: A person . . . crying? A person crying in the distance, at a funeral? Like that lady at the cemetery today who wouldn't *shut up?*

Beat.

Will you come take your boots off? Come on: come take your boots off now.

SARAH JEAN: But, Mom, can you hear it?

CARMEN: Hear what.

Two or three beats of SARAH JEAN staring at CARMEN.

SARAH JEAN: Can you hear it.

CARMEN: No?

SARAH JEAN: CAN YOU HEAR IT!

CARMEN: HEAR WHAT NO I CAN'T HEAR IT?

SARAH JEAN: HEY CAN YOU HEAR IT!

SARAH JEAN starts violently kicking her boots off and wrecking anything in her reach. She doesn't look at her mother. CARMEN starts trying to grab SARAH JEAN, and SARAH JEAN writhes away.

CARMEN: STOP IT! NO STOP IT. STOP IT. / STOP IT.

SARAH JEAN: YOU STOP IT YOU STOP IT. YOU STOP IT. YOU STOP IT. YOU STOP IT.

Pause.

There is a standoff: CARMEN and SARAH JEAN stare at each other, panting.

It sounds like . . . like whispering . . . ?

Beat.

CARMEN: Yeah.

SARAH JEAN: Yeah.

Pause.

They listen.

CARMEN: There: that . . . low register of . . . ?

SARAH JEAN: Yeah.

SARAH JEAN and CARMEN both stand still and listen.

SARAH JEAN is smiling.

Pause.

CARMEN: That's the furnace.

CARMEN exits.

SARAH JEAN stops smiling.

Transition.

Scene Eight.

SARAH JEAN regards us.

SARAH JEAN smiles—with difficulty—at the audience.

Musical phrases and textual phrases intertwine, trading off with one another, dialogue filling the pauses in the music.

Finale Part 1.

SARAH JEAN: My mom . . . drifted her car into the guardrail on a highway.

Beat.

She was in the ICU this week, holding on, and I've been living in the hospital waiting room.

Beat.

But, uh . . .

Beat.

But she died.

Beat.

It's not certain if she . . . fell asleep or if she . . . did it . . . to herself, so . . .

Beat.

I've been trying to arrange her funeral. I asked her once what kind of funeral she wanted and all she said was: "I don't know," and then: "No lilies." I talked to the funeral home about it. I took a cab home.

Beat. "Finale Part 1" music ends.

I should go and call K'an, and tell him I found a funeral home I like. And I should go . . . call back the cemetery, and I—I'm upset about . . . my big blond American friend is right, isn't she? I'm very . . . fucked up about love—and it's just—it's so . . . sickening that she knows that about me, but somehow I don't . . . know that . . . about myself, and I keep thinking about . . . my dad and his . . . theory of time and all the . . . *(gestures)* . . . hoopla about it after he died . . . for some . . . reason that . . . ?

SARAH JEAN twitches her hand, listening to the music.

Music phrases and textual phrases intertwine, trading off with one another.

Finale Part 2.

As the music plays, SARAH JEAN *thinks very, very hard, twitching her fingers. Then:*

Yeah: Dad went . . . through his whole life . . . thinking . . . time was just a persistent illusion, and then he was jarred by . . . death, in his case it was the approach of death, and "what if time isn't mathematical: what if the old physics are wrong," "what if the universe isn't fixed and change is possible," and yeah, yeah: you can suddenly know that the way in which you see . . . some . . . thing . . . You can know that some thing you're fucked up about: some thing you thought was . . . fake, some thing you didn't listen to, that you thought had no meaning is . . .

Beat.

Is real.

SARAH JEAN looks at us.

It's real.

Music.

ELLIOT and CARMEN are there.

CARMEN: *(very low and gently, at the level of a whisper)* . . . Elliot . . . Elliot . . . Elliot . . . Elliot . . . Elliot . . . Elliot . . . *(repeat until:)*

ELLIOT's eyes close—love.

SARAH JEAN turns to us. She smiles at us. Maybe she cries: relief.

"Finale Part 2" music ends.

SARAH JEAN: It is . . . real.

End play.

Acknowledgements.

Lee Smolin, the renowned theoretical physicist, acted as the consulting physicist on *Infinity*. It would be hard to overestimate his influence. We have—with Lee's permission—lifted ideas directly from his book, *Time Reborn: From the Crisis in Physics to the Future of the Universe*, and incorporated them into the text. Lee wrote an eight-page biography for Elliot (the theoretical-physicist character in *Infinity*) that I have used to shape the play, and he has collaborated with me on the writing of the physics in the piece, revising the text with me. I am infinitely grateful to him. Huge thanks are due to Ross Manson, who commissioned this work and conceived of it with me. He has profoundly influenced its meanings. Thank you to Richard Rose and Andrea Romaldi for their (as always) deft dramaturgy. Thanks also to Kate Alton, Paul Braunstein, Njo Kong Kie, Isabelle Ly, Mariel Marshall, Haley McGee, Rebecca Picherack, Teresa Przybylski, Amy Rutherford, and Andréa Tyniec for their beautiful work and dramaturgical contributions to the text.

Hannah Moscovitch is the acclaimed author of *East of Berlin*, *Little One & Other Plays*, *The Russian Play*, *This Is War*, and several other works. She has written for TV, radio, and opera. Hannah has won multiple awards for her work, and was the first Canadian woman and Canadian playwright to win the prestigious Windham-Campbell Award and the first playwright to ever win the Trillium Book Award. She lives in Halifax.

Njo Kong Kie was born in Indonesia and grew up in Macau where he received his musical education from the Academia de Música São Pio X. Long-serving pianist and music director of La La La Human Steps, Kong Kie gave close to 600 performances with the company throughout Canada and abroad between 1996 and 2012. Music from his album of original compositions *Picnic in the Cemetery* has been used on the stages of the Nederlands Dans Theater, Ballet de l'Opéra national du Rhin, Hubbard Street Dance Chicago, Ballet British Columbia, and the Singapore Dance Theatre. He has created original soundtracks for the Silesian Dance Theatre (Poland), Point View Art Association (Macau), and for choreographer Anne Plamondon (Montreal) and filmmaker Alejandro Alvarez. His original creations for the stage include operas and musical theatre, such as *knotty together* (with Anna Chatterton), *La Señorita Mundo* (with Kico Gonzalez-Risso), *The Futures Market* (with Douglas Rodger), *Mr. Shi and His Lover* (with Wong Teng Chi), and the non-text based concert theatre *Picnic in the Cemetery*. He calls Toronto home.

First edition: January 2017
Printed and bound in Canada by Imprimerie Gauvin, Gatineau

Cover design by Monnet Design

202-269 Richmond St. W.
Toronto, ON
M5V 1X1

416.703.0013
info@playwrightscanada.com
www.playwrightscanada.com
@playcanpress

A **bundled** eBook edition is available
with the purchase of this print book.

CLEARLY PRINT YOUR NAME ABOVE IN UPPER CASE

Instructions to claim your eBook edition:
1. Download the BitLit app for Android or iOS
2. Write your name in **UPPER CASE** above
3. Use the BitLit app to submit a photo
4. Download your eBook to any device

MIX
Paper from
responsible sources
FSC® C100212